Malls

The Sound of M

By Cynthia Amoroso and Peg Ballard

Map of the Mall

1. clothes
2. shoes
3. pets
4. toys
5. books
6. food
7. movies

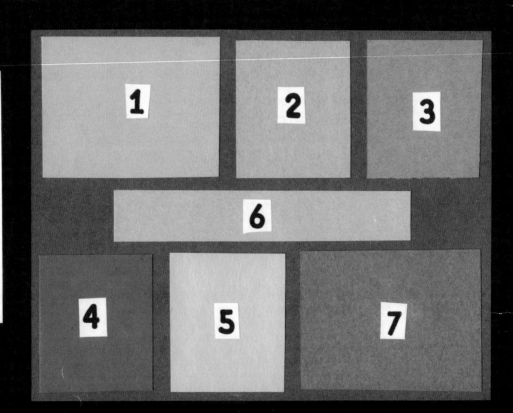

I made a map
of the mall.

The map of the mall shows us where to go.

5

6

The map of the mall shows us where the clothes are.

The map of the mall shows us where the shoes are.

The map of the mall shows us where the pets are.

The map of the mall shows us where the toys are.

13

14

The map of the mall shows us where the books are.

The map of the mall shows us where the food is.

food
court

The map of the mall shows us where the movies are.

The map of the mall shows us where to go.

Word List:

made

mall

map

movies

Note to Parents and Educators

The books in this series are based on current research, which supports the idea that our brains are pattern-detectors rather than rules-appliers. This means children learn to read easier when they are taught the familiar spelling patterns found in English. As children encounter more complex words, they have greater success in figuring out these words by using the spelling patterns.

Throughout the series, the texts provide the reader with the opportunity to practice and apply knowledge of the sounds in natural language. The books introduce sounds using familiar onsets and *rimes*, or spelling patterns, for reinforcement.

For example, the word *cat* might be used to present the short "a" sound, with the letter *c* being the onset and "_at" being the rime. This approach provides practice and reinforcement of the short "a" sound, as there are many familiar words made with the "_at" rime.

The stories and accompanying photographs in this series are based on time-honored concepts in children's literature: well-written, engaging texts and colorful, high-quality photographs combine to produce books that children want to read again and again.

Dr. Peg Ballard
Minnesota State University, Mankato

childsworld.com

Published by The Child's World®
1980 Lookout Drive • Mankato, MN 56003-1705
800-599-READ • www.childsworld.com

ACKNOWLEDGMENTS
The Child's World®: Mary Swensen, Publishing Director
The Design Lab: Design
Michael Miller: Editing

PHOTO CREDITS
© Aviahuismanphotography/Dreamstime.com: 14;
Clearvista/Dreamstime.com: 10; Danie Nel/Shutterstock.
com: 5; fiphoto/Shutterstock.com: 6, 9; Ivy Photos/
Shutterstock.com: 21; Marcel Poncu/Dreamstime.com:
17; Mary Swensen: 2; Mikhail Rulkov/Shutterstock.com:
13; TravnikovStudio/Shutterstock.com: cover; Tyler Olson/
Shutterstock.com: 18

ISBN 9781503809093
LCCN 2015958476

Printed in the United States of America
Mankato, MN
June, 2016
PA02310

ABOUT THE AUTHORS

Cynthia Amoroso holds undergraduate
degrees in English and elementary education, and graduate degrees in curriculum
and instruction as well as educational ad-
ministration. She is currently an assistant
superintendent in a suburban metropolitan
school district. Cynthia's past roles include
teacher, assistant principal, district reading
coordinator, director of curriculum and
instruction, and curriculum consultant.
She has extensive experience in reading,
literacy, curriculum development, pro-
fessional development, and continuous
improvement processes.

Dr. Peg Ballard holds a PhD from Purdue
University and is an associate professor
in the Department of Elementary & Early
Childhood Education at Minnesota State
University, Mankato. Her areas of expertise
are assessment, interventions, and
response to intervention. Dr. Ballard teaches
online graduate courses in the K–12 reading
licensure and master's program along with
reading interventions in the undergraduate
teacher preparation program.